Storm Clouds Over Party Shoes

❦❦❦❦❦❦❦❦❦❦❦❦❦

ETIQUETTE PROBLEMS
for the ILL-BRED WOMAN

Sheila Norgate

PRESS GANG PUBLISHERS
VANCOUVER

The Publisher gratefully acknowledges financial assistance
from the Book Publishing Industry Development Program of
the Department of Canadian Heritage, the Cultural Services
Branch, Province of British Columbia, and from the Canada
Council for the Arts.

CANADIAN CATALOGUING IN PUBLICATION DATA

Norgate, Sheila
  Storm clouds over party shoes

  ISBN 0-88974-080-1
  I. Etiquette for women—Humor. I. Title.
BJ1843.N67 1997   395.1′44′0207   C97-910582-X

Editing by Barbara Kuhne
Design by Val Speidel
Photograph of author page 77 by Patricia Norgate
Printed by Kings Times Industries Ltd.
Printed and bound in Hong Kong

Press Gang Publishers
225 East 17th Avenue, Suite 101
Vancouver, British Columbia
V5V 1A6 Canada
TEL: 604/876-7787 FAX: 604/876-7892

Acknowledgements

Being a *nice girl*, I want to thank everyone I've ever met for fear of leaving someone out. But I simply must thank: Press Gang Publishers (Barbara Kuhne and Della McCreary) for their gentle stewardship and fierce commitment to the words and images of women; Val Speidel for her brilliant design and expansive vision; Robin Laurence for bringing her clear and passionate voice to the foreword; the Community Arts Council of Vancouver for sponsoring the first exhibition of the 'Etiquette' work; my feminist women writers' group, "Sex, Death and Madness," for their accompaniment along the creative path and for never quite figuring out how to operate our cheesy little timer; my cherished friends and patrons (you know who you are) who have supported my work in thought and deed for these many years; and my partner, Martine, for her unbridled enthusiasm, precious insight, and enduring love. My deep gratitude to Catherine D. for helping me reconstruct the Statue of Liberty even when I wasn't sure we had all the pieces.

For my mother, Patricia Norgate (1922–1995),

English war bride, embittered nice girl, and stifled creative genius,

who did not live to see this work.

Contents

Beyond Niceness

by ROBIN LAURENCE

When I first encountered an exhibition of Sheila Norgate's etiquette series — the works reproduced in these pages — I was immediately caught. Caught in a net of observation so finely woven with humour, irony and absurdity, so subtly crafted with gentle colour and anachronistic type, and so unassuming in scale that it didn't feel like a net. In fact, I laughed, smiled and chuckled my way around the gallery where the work was hanging, then began taking notes for a review. But truly, I had been caught.

Norgate's show was called "It's More Fun When You Know the Rules: Etiquette Problems for Girls," after a 1935 book of the same title. With its emphasis on good manners and "good breeding," the work speaks to a particular order of gender inequity, of genteel sexism, of oppression within niceness. It speaks to the stifled condition of white, middle-class North American women and girls in the years before and following the Second World War. Yet the attitudes expressed here — women accommodating themselves to the expectations of men, women making themselves neat, sweet, servile, slim, dim, pretty, quiet, uncomplaining and as absorbent as blotters — continue to be felt. And notions of inadequacy continue to be passed through generations of women. Few art shows have stimulated the reactions of pained amusement, of chagrined recognition, that

Norgate's did. The empathetic responses of viewers—female and male, old and young—filled the comments book in the gallery.

Sheila Norgate was born in Toronto, five years into the Baby Boom and three girls into a large, middle-class family. Her parents' marriage was unhappy and home life was charged with anxiety, emotional abuse and the threat of physical violence. Humour very early became a survival strategy for Norgate, a way, she says, of "laundering" her feelings and endearing herself to others, insuring a kind of shelter in an otherwise unsafe environment.

After studying psychology and sociology—not art—at university, Norgate drifted into a career in banking, moving to Vancouver in 1975, and to Victoria in 1981. It was in Victoria in the early 1980s that personal crisis impelled her to come out of the banking closet as an artist. A debilitating chronic illness confined her to bed, and the art-making triggered by this confinement and loss of control coincided with psychotherapy Norgate was undertaking. Much of what she was struggling to achieve in therapy—self-realization, the recovery of a voice that had long been silenced—began to be enacted in her art.

For years, on special occasions, Norgate had been producing small watercolours as gifts for friends and family—but without ever making a commitment to art for its (or her) own sake. Highly symbolic in the self-effacing pattern of her early, amateur art-making was the process of working on her kitchen table, then clearing away all evidence of that work so that the table could resume its domestic function. Equally symbolic was Norgate's purchase, in 1983, of her own drafting table, a space dedicated to art, not dinner. On this table, Norgate's work evolved from gentle little landscapes in muted and melancholy hues—greys, browns, ochres, mossy greens—to floral scenes in colours she considered "outrageous"—brilliant reds, blues and yellows.

But even as Norgate's colours and brushwork became more assertive, the subject matter remained safe and safely dependent on sketches or photographs, and the pictures remained untitled. The appearance of a hard-edged abstraction in late 1984, "The anger seems to be everywhere," was the first signal of darkness rising up beneath the bright decorum, of angry and creative impulses emerging directly from Norgate's psyche. It was also, with its explicit title, the first hint of the important connection between images and text in Norgate's art practice. Her untitled floral works in 1985 were something of a retreat, but they were also a forecasting of what would become her most enduring and iconic motif: the heart. Watercolours of blood-red flowers on slender green stems—the red bleeding wetly into the white paper, the stems so thin and tenuous that the flowers threaten to break away from them completely— anticipate later, equally brilliant images of poppy-red hearts in fields of green, hearts on stems and hearts untethered, floating off into the night sky. The sky of passionate imaginings.

In the fall of 1985, Norgate enrolled in art classes at a local college. Although illness caused her to withdraw after only one semester, she took away with her the knowledge of relief-printing or block-printing techniques, which she employed in her work for nearly a decade. (Describing herself as a "primitive printmaker," Norgate cut her designs into Styrofoam, the lightest, cheapest and least prestigious of printing materials.) Combining watercolour painting with block printing, Norgate produced a series of works with repetitive heart motifs and expressive titles like "The heart lying down is still a heart," "One must always speak gently to an unfolding heart," and "A heart kept always on the floor can never know there are windows." Formally, these works suggest inspiration in sleek Pop Art and cool Minimalism. The titles, however, set up a quite different dynamic, one in which the heart functions as an expressive symbol for self-realization, for what Norgate sees as "a passionate involvement in life, the courage to act from the heart and not just the head."

Again, Norgate's gentle work anticipated tougher images and strategies: the head-heart dichotomy of her late 1980s works foreshadowed her "Nice Girl-Bad Girl" opposition in the 1990s. In "My heart held a party to which I was invited but couldn't go because I was afraid I'd see someone I knew," a mixed media piece completed in 1986, there is a sense of natural impulse stifled by propriety, ardent feeling stifled by fear of social censure. And again, in "My heart had been arrested for causing a disturbance and I was called downtown to pick it out of a line-up," the heart seems to symbolize socially unacceptable behaviour. An ongoing and significant theme in her art, Norgate has said, is her "struggle to come to consciousness from a place of repression." The heart (and later, the Bad Girl) signifies the shaking off of a condition that is both personal and political. As Norgate played out this struggle, she also developed a more integral relationship between image and text: she began to incorporate words directly into her pictures, a natural progression from her increasingly long, increasingly narrative titles. Words had become as important to the "reading" of her art as images—and Norgate had found her voice.

In 1990, Norgate began a series of works describing the behaviours of "Nice Girls," using images found amongst the remnants of mid-century popular culture, including a sweet, blank face from a 1940s logo of a waitress. Waitresses serve — and the Nice Girl serves too. She is an image of self-effacement, self-abnegation, self-denial. (For Norgate, part of becoming a "reformed Nice Girl" was giving up what she saw as the Nice-Girl medium of watercolour and employing acrylic paint instead. Watercolour is "exacting and unforgiving," Norgate says. It disallows mistakes—or even changes.) In her accommodation to social expectation, her invisibility, inaudibility and inability to claim her own space, Norgate's Nice Girl anticipates the women whose circumscribed lives are explored in the etiquette works.

By contrast, Norgate's Bad Girl series articulates the condition of women who "take up space." Bad Girls are seen and heard; they demand attention; they declare their own sexuality. They are not bad but whole. In Norgate's words, "Bad is the judgement that society has about any woman who wants what she wants when she wants it." Part of that judgement, of course, is directed towards lesbians, and in her Bad Girl series, as in other works, Norgate occasionally alludes to her own sexual orientation. Being a lesbian has informed and inflected—but not principally directed—the course of her feminist art.

Around the time Norgate began imaging the tussles between mind and heart, nice behaviour and bad, she also began employing geometric motifs like zigzags, lines and dots, often incorporating them into wide borders around the central images and texts. (The designs of many of Norgate's works are reminiscent of Middle Eastern carpets.) Consciously, she was drawn to decorative elements found in the work of artists like Henri Matisse and David Hockney. Unconsciously, she was aligning her practice with the applied arts and crafts of anonymous women artists throughout history and around the world. The intimate scale and decorative appearance of many of Norgate's works run counter to an aggressive and aggrandizing masculine aesthetic.

In 1992, Norgate moved back to Vancouver, and in 1994, she found *It's More Fun When You Know the Rules*, an etiquette book that spelled out many of the manners and mores by which she had been raised. Her surprise and amusement at this discovery were quickly followed by anger and indignation at the inequities this book encoded. Working again on a small scale, using mixed media (acrylic paint, collage and hand-tinted laser prints), she combined images appropriated from women's magazines of the pre- and post-war era with rules of etiquette transcribed on her old, manual typewriter (complete with botched, over-typed and off-register letters). Juxtaposing found images with verbatim words of admonishment, Norgate has carefully reconstructed—and deconstructed—a text of gender conditioning. The results are, as you see here, at once hilarious and horrifying, real and ridiculous. But in exposing these rules as ridiculous, in engaging and enraging us, Norgate has shown us how to dispose of them. Her humour has snagged these silly strictures, filled them with helium and released them into oblivion. It's a project in which both Nice Girls and Bad Girls can rejoice.

Storm Clouds
Over Party Shoes

Etiquette as Emergency Preparedness or Modern Mental Hygiene

*A*re you a good girl whose good times have sometimes been spoiled—simply because at the crucial moment you didn't quite know what to do or to say? If you are—or if you want to make sure that you won't be that kind of a girl when you are a little older—this book is especially for you. (1935)

*E*tiquette is a great deal more than a social nicety; it is a part of modern mental hygiene. It is a wonderful comfort to have islands of certainty to swim to when one plunges out from the self into society. (1941)

A man should know at once whether you are what is known as a nice girl. You will have a much better time if you are. (1941)

*I*t is a mark of extreme good breeding to be able to meet all emergencies calmly and without uncontrolled anger or excitement. (1923)

*T*he woman of dignity protects her poise by doing the thoughtful thing in the first place. (1941)

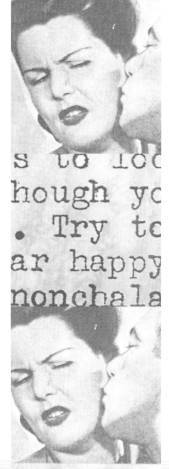

*W*hen a girl will take the trouble to prepare herself to be entertaining, gay, and amusing, she will not lose many dates by not petting. (1941)

*D*on't take the lead or insist upon spending an evening the way you had hoped you would. Make people feel that they and their ideas are just the thing you have been hoping for—and isn't it nice you found them tonight? (1941)

*T*he sight of a woman constantly pulling up her shoulder straps is almost as offensive as straps which are not absolutely clean, though perhaps not so distasteful as the sight of a woman forever pulling down a girdle. Get dressed properly at home and then stop fussing! (1940 [a])

Smile Though Your Heart Is Breaking

A lady will endure agonies rather than be rude. (1941)

And whether you feel any enthusiasm for your date's team or not, let him think you do. Disinterest or lack of loyalty to his school is as bad or worse than lack of knowledge of the sport. (1965)

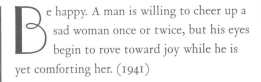

Be happy. A man is willing to cheer up a sad woman once or twice, but his eyes begin to rove toward joy while he is yet comforting her. (1941)

No matter what goes wrong, [a hostess] must cover it as best she can and at the same time cover the fact that she is covering it. (1965)

The chest held high is a sign of inner well-being. Even if there is heart-break and sorrow, the sooner we show the gallant attitude, the sooner there will be healing. Also, we should not burden the world with symbols of our own difficulties—the drooping chest and crestfallen posture of defeat. (1941)

*N*ow perhaps some of you will find that you will arrive at your next dance and still be something of a wallflower . . . Even though you may be terribly hurt, anyone who notices at all will like you better for being a good sport and covering up your real feelings. (1935)

Ever so slight
a change will
help. If you
could scream
at the sight
of one more
dish to wash,
go sweep the
porch.

Even when you
aren't having
a good time it
helps to look
as though you
were. Try to
appear happy
and nonchalant.
Very few boys
like earnest-
looking girls.

Even though a girl may loathe cooking, she should make an effort to cater to her husband's likes and dislikes and to make meals appetizing and interesting.

Charm and beauty are the
heritage of woman and the
world expects it of her.

The Art of Conversation: Telling It Like It's Not

A man fears a sharp-tongued woman. She ought to fear herself. (1941)

If you are talking to a man, another helpful gambit is to ask advice . . . in fact, it is safe to ask his opinion on almost anything. (1965)

It is cynical advice, but it is as true today as it was in the day of Cleopatra that a man is rarely bored if you talk—but with some intelligence—about him. (1965)

A tried and true plan is for the girl to start a conversation that centres around the boy himself, something concerned with *his* hobbies or *his* plans for the future, or *his* ideas or characteristics. We all like to discuss ourselves and I am inclined to think boys like to talk about themselves even more than girls do. (1935)

Once during an evening is enough for a woman to state a definite and unqualified opinion—and even then it should be something constructive or a defense of someone or something. (1941)

A clever woman will not long let a man remain in the role of audience. No matter how perfect her performance may be, it cannot possibly be fascinating enough to keep his mind off himself. (1941)

A wise woman sees to it that a man associates her with gaiety over his wit, with breathlessness over his stories, with wonder at his daring vision and dreams. (1941)

It seems that a girl must always start the flow of conversation, but once she has the conversational ice broken she need only say "isn't that interesting?" or "do go on" a few times and almost any man will be delighted. (1940 [a])

Men are wonderful creatures. The grandest of them are satisfied with so little—it seems a pity for them not to have that little. (1941)

They like a girl who can make them feel **intelligent** by starting a conversation on a subject that interests him. There was never a better line for any girl than the good old "aren't you wonderful?" Don't try to impress him with what you know but let him impress you with how clever he is. The men will beat a path to your door.

The intelligent woman will listen as though she cares to her husband's problems at the office.

If You Must Think:
What You Know Can Hurt You

The girl just out of college with a fairly good job runs the risk of becoming unpopular—not because she can't talk, but because she thinks she knows more than her men friends . . . and your average man doesn't like a "strong-minded" woman. (1940 [a])

If you *must* think . . . (1962)

Be ready, willing, and able to play with your love; but beat him at his own game—never! It blows a boy to be beaten—by you. So play well for zest, but not too well for his comfort. (n.d.)

What she says is nothing very important; charm of expression and manner can convey a far more gracious welcome than the most elaborate phrases, which as a matter of fact, should be studiously avoided. (1965)

Girls with brains are all right but the brains musn't be too evident.

When a boy takes you to a dance or
anywhere, don't dash on ahead and
climb into taxicabs or cars unaided.
Wait for the boy to open the car
door for you and let him help you
in. It isn'ta question of whether
or not you are able to get in and
out of cars without assistance.
Of course you are. You can open
doors too..but when you are accom-
panied by a boy, you just don't..
you must let him do these things
for you. He will feel a great deal
more comfortable, more pleased with
you and himself.

5

The Business Woman: Why Can't a Woman Be More Like a Man?

Never doubt that a keen interviewer will see the contents of your purse if you open it, and he may believe that there is a definite relation between its neatness and that of your desk or file. (1940)

Be sure that your skirt is long enough and full enough that you can sit on any office chair with dignity, confident that not too great a length of stocking is exposed. You are warned against not wearing girdles, brassieres and slips even in the summer. It is obvious that no employer is going to bother to admit you to his organization and try to correct such omissions later. (1940)

It's still a man's world and the girl who thinks otherwise is playing a losing, if gallant, game. (1941)

The clever business woman realizes that she is on ground long held sacred to men and that, while she must remain a lady in the finest sense of the word, she must not expect to find drawing-room manners in an office. (1940 [a])

The woman who would be a success in business, must remember that she cannot do justice to the business of the moment, if she is wondering whether her skirt falls just right, whether her blouse is still crisply laundered, whether the colors she is wearing are not too bright. She becomes embarrassed, flustered—and she fails to do justice to whatever should have been claiming her attention. (1923)

The idea is to treat the men in your office (and more especially your superiors) as impersonally as possible. You can do it, no matter how attractive and pretty you are. Any girl can who really wants to, or who uses her head. (1935)

Women who work must learn not to waste their employers' time, and employers should know that the effect on morale of a ten-minute make-up repair or coffee break more than makes up in increased efficiency for the actual loss in time. (1965)

*A*t home and at parties you may be accustomed to having a roomful of males scramble to their feet and wait until you are seated. Don't expect any such goings on in the office. (1935)

*S*he can't have her cake of gracious courtesies and eat the sweet of independence at the same time. (1941)

*T*here is nothing more conducive to respect, trust and honor in business than quiet tastes—in clothes as in everything else. One instinctively respects the young lady who is smartly attired in dark, simple clothes, ideally adapted to the business environment. How much more sensible she looks, how much more eager one is to trust her with confidential information, with responsible duties, than the flippant person who wears gaudy clothes! (1923)

Every business man likes a wo
efficient, just as he likes a
the distance without any dang

n who is neat, impersonal, and
automobile that is ready to go
of breaking down.

By her manners and her dress,
a woman determines her place,
and the women who are careless
of their appearance and their
standards are the ones who are
hindering theprogress of women
toward the goal of perfect
womanhood.

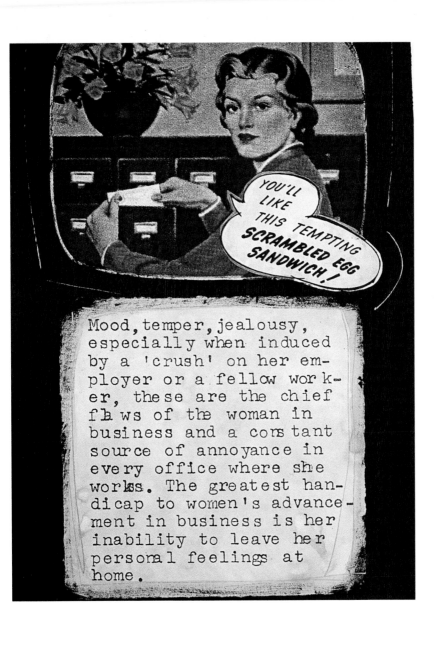

6

Short, Tall, Fat, Thin:
Some of the Most Fascinating
Girls Are Homely

The overplump girl looks more slender in dull fabrics and quiet colours . . . the butterfly looks very dashing in brilliant shades, but gray is, no doubt, more becoming to an elephant. (1935)

A straight spine and well-poised head are as important when a woman is seated in her car as when she is in a box at the opera. (1941)

Prominent, floppy buttocks are far from pretty. A gentle curve is natural and pleasing, but beware of protuberances. They spoil the hang of your skirts and ruin your silhouette. (1935)

Perhaps the commonest and homeliest walking fault of all, especially where women are concerned, is the trick of walking with the hips thrust out behind, a posture peculiarity that inevitably results when the knees are stiff. This trait not only makes you broad in the beam—which is bad enough—but it also throws you into that waggling walk which is such a sad but familiar rear-end spectacle. (1923)

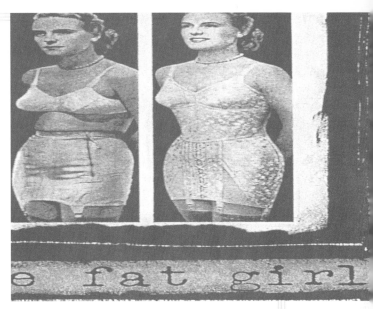

The thin woman has a great friend in taffeta. (1941)

For the thin woman, an easy, graceful manner is most important. When she develops such a manner, and combines it with the fluffiest and most frilly of feminine fashions, one will see how very charming she can be. The too-stout woman faces a more difficult problem. She must carefully consider each detail of her dress, making sure that it does not in any way accentuate her fleshiness . . . It is not deplorable to be stout, but it certainly is deplorable to dress in a manner which emphasizes that stoutness. (1923)

The fat girl must give up wearing shorts and sl... in public.

Hips are a story in themselves, the storm centre for figures. (1947)

There is nothing worse for your figure, or for your clothes, than wrong sitting. Your skirts soon get baggy, and no matter how slender you may be, in time you widen out alarmingly across the hips. (1935)

Perhaps the worst single thing you can do to spoil your looks is to let your knees spread apart. (1947)

Even housework has great possibilities for giving you a beautiful figure if you learn to use the right muscles when you sweep, stoop, and walk upstairs. (1935)

The plainest girl will have some redeeming feature. She usually has several good features. I know one girl whose sole claim to distinction is her well-modulated voice. She's frankly not much to look at, but her voice is so charming and her conversation so interesting that she gains and holds your interest. (1940 [a])

The really homely girl has a harder time, socially, at the start. But in the long run, I wonder if she isn't likely to come off better than the girl who is so pretty that she never exerts herself to be entertaining. About the time that the merely pretty girl is getting a little faded and ineffective, the homely one may have made herself into a fascinating person. (1935)

Learn to drive your body as you learned to drive a car. (1947)

Attractive looks are an asset, certainly, but a bright, responsive personality is far more friend-making than great beauty—even for a girl. (1965)

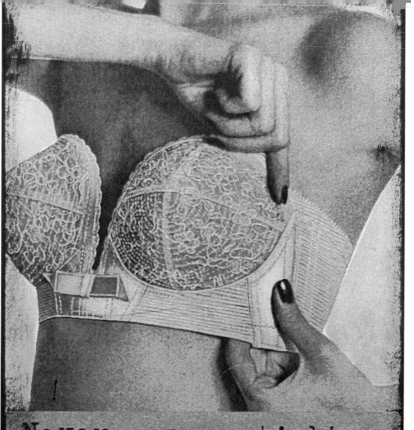

Never wear a tight
brassiere under any
circumstances for
that will break down
the muscles in your
breasts, and in a few
years they will be
sagging and ugly.

IMAGINE...

Just a month ago I was ashamed of the way I looked!

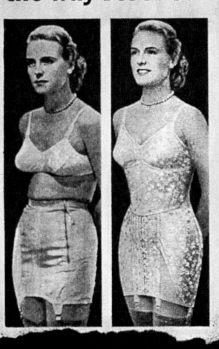

The fat girl

must give up wearing shorts and slacks in public.

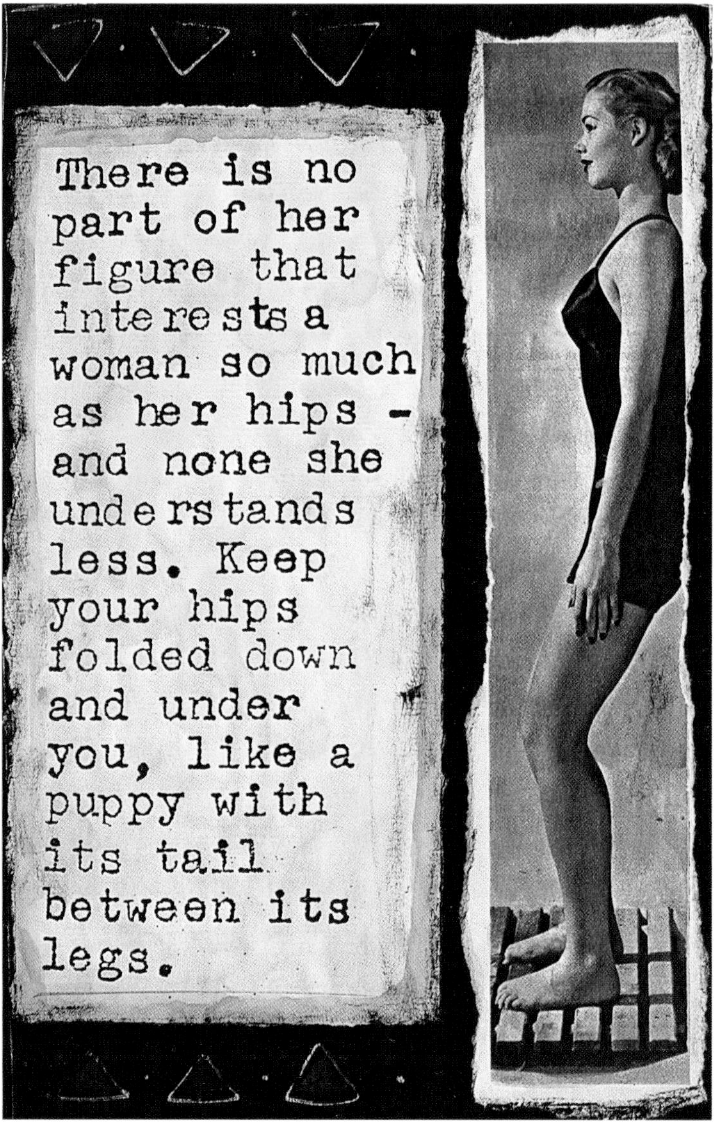

There is no
part of her
figure that
interests a
woman so much
as her hips -
and none she
understands
less. Keep
your hips
folded down
and under
you, like a
puppy with
its tail
between its
legs.

In order to balance the head
evenly as well as for the
sake of symmetry, it should
be so perfectly poised aloft
that you could at any moment
balance a saucer on it without preliminary adjustment.

Exercise 3

You are never guilty of course, of
in the corridor or classroom. Inste
trim by systematic exercise that y

teral Bending

ing around pulling down your girdl
you keep your figure so firm and
don't need a girdle.

7

Making Up
Is Hard To Do

Make-up: a friend of the beautiful woman and a veritable life-saver for her less fortunate sister. (1941)

If you are not a pretty girl, there are other possibilities for you. You can be exquisite in your grooming, you can dress with skill and taste, and thus bring out your best points and submerge your worst ones. You can make yourself look distinguished, or interesting, or jolly, or lovable. (1935)

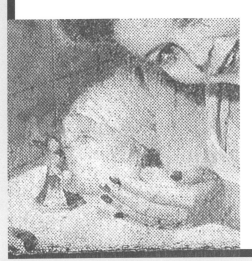

A well-mannered girl, for her part, may powder her nose or touch a lipstick to her lips, but she does not comb her hair, file her nails, or give her complexion a general going over in public. (1940 [a])

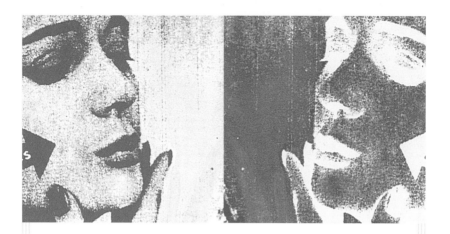

There are many ways in which girls offend unconsciously. A girl's manners may be polite, her character sweet, yet she spoils it all by unclean, though brightly painted fingernails, a soiled powder puff, or an untidy, bulging pocketbook. (1940 [a])

Eye make-up, if used, should also be applied with discretion. A heavy outline intended to enlarge the eye can, in reality, destroy the natural line and appear nothing short of grotesque. (1965)

dry "crow's feet"

tense frown-marks

"peel-y" patches

Always remember that a mask can never take the place of a face. The face of a clown is grotesque for it is meant to be. If cosmetics are to add to beauty they must be the allies, not the enemies of nature.

The woman who smears
her face with cream
and rolls her hair in
curlers before going
to bed is not a sight
that many husbands
can endure.

8

A Happy Marriage: The Wife's Part

It is up to you as a girl to know what is expected of boys and men as well as of yourself for men do depend on women to promote and maintain certain standards and ideals. Even though they grumble over what they call our fussiness about etiquette and conventions, most of them are secretly proud to have wives or daughters or sisters or girlfriends who know what is correct. (1935)

There is room for originality, and by the same token, for freakishness in women's dress, and therefore the greater responsibility is hers. (1923)

A woman can civilize a husband if necessary so that he is fit for human society by disarming approval, which will gradually make him aware of his good effects and he will discard the unattractive ones. Sometimes it is a slow and wearying process, but worth it in the end if she means to stay married to him. (1941)

The wife who prepares and sees her husband off to work in a dirty bathrobe, with hair uncombed and face unwashed, sends him off with a thoroughly unflattering picture of her in his mind. No

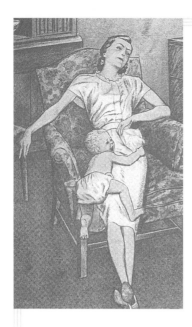

wonder many a man has found his neat, efficient, pretty secretary more appealing than his unkempt, uncaring wife! (1965)

She who changes her dress and fixes her hair for her husband's homecoming is sure to greet him with greater charm than she who thinks whatever she happens to have on is good enough. The very fact of *looking* more attractive makes one feel less tired and therefore more charming and better company (1965)

The slovenly housewife is the one who greets her returning husband with a lament about her hard day's work—and with that she breaks a link in the chain which binds him to her. (1940 [a])

A job may not last a lifetime, but it is always to be hoped that a marriage will. (1948)

It must be admitted that in spite of all the charm which frankness and friendliness give to American women, they are often unwittingly, and most unbecomingly, careless in their attitude toward their husbands. Deference is perhaps too strong a word to describe the perfect attitude, but certainly there should be a noticeable deferring, on the part of the wife, toward the husband as head of the house. A woman can gracefully play second fiddle, but a man who is obviously subordinated to a dominating woman is a pathetic and foolish figure. (1948)

*I*f her husband is the type who enjoys an evening of poker with his friends, the smart wife will cheer him on his way and even offer to provide refreshments for his gang at home when it is his turn to invite them there. She leaves everything in readiness and disappears—completely! But if he is bringing a business acquaintance home, she must be a gracious hostess until after dinner, when she excuses herself, washes up quietly, and goes to her room to leave them to their business discussion. (1965)

*I*t is well to remember that most men, when they think of themselves as husbands, would rather be bored by a wife than embarrassed or fooled by her. (1948)

If a young man wants a wife
in whose daily life he is
always sure to find the fin-
ished task, the tidy mind, and
the organized housekeeping, he
may be quite safe in selecting
her from those whose letters
are well-written, even, and
neat.

When there are three c
and the home is a smal
butler are sufficient.

four grownup daughters
one, one maid and one

Love went packing . . .

Through . . . done for . . . all our dreams and sharing, and our little "love nest" of a home! . . . *Foolish me*—not to realize it was *my* fault our happiness was spoiled. I *thought* I understood about feminine hygiene. But it took my doctor to save the day for us. He pointed out, oh *so* emphatically: "Once-in-a-while care just isn't enough" . . . and told me to use "Lysol" brand disinfectant for douching—always.

For some reason it seems that the bride generally has to make more effort to achieve a successful marriage than the groom.

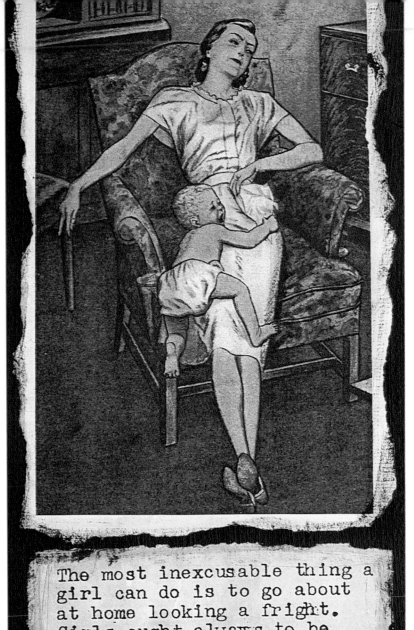

The most inexcusable thing a girl can do is to go about at home looking a fright. Girls ought always to be sweet and attractive in appearance and home is no exception.

9

The Clever Hostess: Happy Is She

The ideal hostess is the one who can make her guests, one and all, feel better satisfied with themselves and the world in general when they leave her home than they did when they arrived. (1923)

No matter whether you have special home duties or not, there is one responsibility that falls on a girl, which you must learn to carry gracefully. You must be responsible for the behaviour of your guests. (1935)

The hostess does not finish eating a course before the last guest has laid down his fork. So long as anyone is eating, she must appear to be accompanying him—even though

she may be merely chasing a single pea round and round her plate. (1941)

Whatever happens, a hostess is always charming and agreeable. Her entire household staff may become demoralized, half her guests may desert her, and it may rain "cats and dogs" over the entire week end, but she remains relaxed and delightful. (1941)

In talk, as on the beach, there is a sharp line between calm confidence and showing off. Many a hostess has loosened a stubborn tongue only to find herself practically unable to stop its wagging—such are the joys and temptations of the thoughtless talker. (1941)

Anything short of unpleasantness is bad manners and a sin against all etiquette. Any sense of strain is unpleasant. The attitude of the hostess quickly permeates a room. It is for this reason, and not because she is too pure to behold evil, that a hostess must never recognize an unpleasantness. (1941)

The greatest pride of the Amer
nd it is to her credit that w
wn against the most aristocra

an hostess is her formal dinner
mention that she can hold her
e families of Europe.

The unthinking hostess will
put two men who are the best
players in town at a table
with one woman who, imagining
herself a wit, thinks of nothing but the next bright remark
she canmake and a second woman
who is beautiful to look at,
but who knows scarcely more
than a child of eight about
bidding.

10

Accessories:
Everything in its Place

Hats may be worn with the daytime dress, but rarely with the cocktail dress and never with the dinner dress. (1965)

Women of good taste adopt only those new fashions that are conservative and not obviously "new." Anything radically different, anything extreme, should be strickly avoided. (1923)

A woman dining alone should always wear her hat into the dining room even if she is a guest of the hotel. (1923)

Don't wear old finery in the house or when going to the beach. (1940 [a])

Don't wear sports gloves with a dress coat or white kid gloves with a sports suit. (1940 [a])

A girl staying at a hotel puts
on her hat in the morning before
leaving her room and probably
keeps it on all day, never giving
it a thought except to stop now and
then in a dressing room to see
that the tilt is still becoming.

For a woman's
evening shoes
there is no
law but that
of beauty.

11

Travel Fashion for Girls

Some women are very attractive in their migrations. Whatever the vehicle in which they are travelling, they invest it with an atmosphere of charm and good breeding by the mere fact of being there. To travel beautifully, casually, and with distinction is an art worth cultivating. (1941)

One thing for the woman who is making her debut flight to remember is that she is not a heroine. She should request no special consideration. (1941)

It is customary in large hotels for lady guests to wear hats at meal time. The only exception would be if they dress for dinner. If she intends to return to her room after lunch, she comes hatless. If she wants to go walking, she may wear her hat. (1940 [a])

A woman alone does not wear a backless low dress and go to the dining room hatless in a great bustling hotel. She would dress inconspicuously and wear a small hat. (1941)

The woman who thinks a hotel is a brier patch where she can hide away all the things she oughtn't to do will find that she might as well have chosen to hide in a show window. (1965)

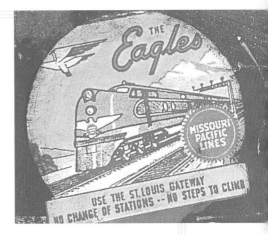

A woman's negligee may be of any type which pleases her, although elaborate, lace-trimmed negligees are not in keeping with shipboard surroundings and ostrich and marabou feathers present a pitiful rather than an alluring spectacle when they have been exposed to salt air and spray. (1941)

A girl makes a mistake to go alone on a cruise. Two or three girls can have a good time together, but the young woman alone is always conspicuous and at a disadvantage. It is not correct for her to be in the ballroom unaccompanied. (1940 [a])

*T*he gloves of a well-dressed woman are never so tight that her hands have the appearance of sausages. (1941)

*P*ossibly the real test of a well-bred woman should be — How does she act after forty-eight hours in a Pullman? (1940 [a])

The grime of travel aside darling, couldn't we do it just once tonight without the gloves? Besides, George and Betty have, and they say we ought to at least give it a try.

norgate

THE Eagles

MISSOURI PACIFIC LINES

USE THE ST. LOUIS GATEWAY
NO CHANGE OF STATIONS -- NO STEPS TO CLIMB

French women, always practical and careful of their appearance, knot a veil over their heads - they do it very smartly - and slip on a pair of loose cotton gloves before going to sleep on a train. This protects the hands from the grime of travel.

Let's see now, there's my navy blue serge for the Lockheed Constellation, my triple sheer 2pc wool suit for the Viscount DC3, and I think maybe a pale organdie wrap with just a touch of bisque crepe for the De Havilland Sea Hornet F20.

The effect that is most attractive is one of neatness, of being stripped down and unencumbered. Veils, flowers, fringes - all these suddenly look impossibly fussy beside the clean lines of an airplane.

PLANES

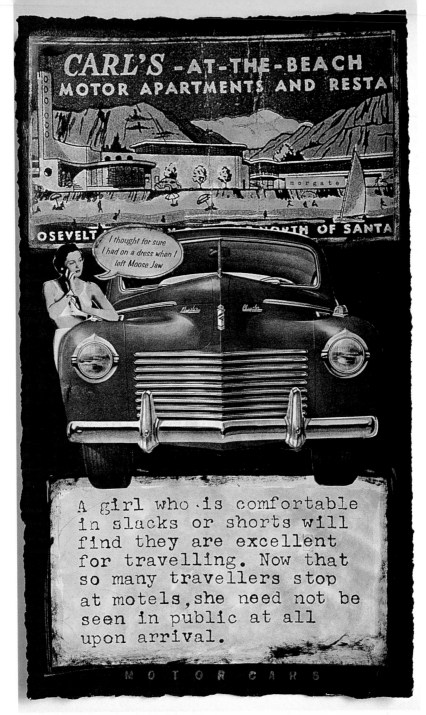

12

The Ill-Bred Woman

Boisterous action in the street car is inexcusable as it is anywhere else. The girl of mirthful disposition who laughs loudly may not be doing it to attract attention to herself but merely to give vent to her gay spirits, but it is most unattractive. (1923)

Never encourage stories that are risqué. (1948)

Never drink enough alcohol to be even slightly affected by it. "She can certainly hold her liquor" is not a compliment. (1948)

Silence is preferred to an uncontrolled gushing of words. (1941)

It is extremely bad taste to wear in public, clothes that depart widely from the accepted norm. Any clothes which make an obvious bid for public attention are offensive evidence of indiscrimination and exhibitionism. (1948)

The woman who looks as though she had jumped into her clothes quickly, dashed off to the office without glancing in the mirror, and then forgotten all about straightening her hat and belt, is a slattern. Broadly speaking, any woman is a slattern who is not scrupulously careful in her attire, who does not show by her very appearance that she is well-groomed, well cared for. (1923)

So that we shall not be saying one thing with our lips and another with our bodies, let's assume the gallant posture as well as the gallant mental attitude. Chests up! The wallflower, almost always, has a low chest and a bad posture. (1941)

The right repose is glamorous and fascinating. The wrong inaction is deadly. Never indulge in blank repose where there are other people. (1941)

No one who wishes to be considered mentally comfortable would cross her legs and then twist the top foot a second time around the lower leg. Such things are stunts that should be reserved for the circus. (1941)

If young girls could hear men discuss women and their ways, they would cling to convention like a limpet to its rock. (1948)

The desire to attract
attention has no place
in the world of good
breeding. Who wishes
to be stared at, re-
marked upon, openly
admired, if not the
ill-bred woman.

13

She Who Laughs Lasts

by SHEILA NORGATE

I f nostalgia is something one must earn over time, then I am at a loss to explain the fact that I have been fiercely nostalgic for as long as I can remember—even before I could have accumulated enough memory to warrant reminiscence. It is the pull backward in time that I have struggled with all of my life as though swimming against some deep and inevitable tide.

My loyalty to the past is explainable only in terms of what it promised but could not possibly provide. I was born in 1950, the third in a disappointing string of girls. In what I would later identify as an uncharacteristic dash towards the future, I emerged from the birth canal practically unannounced, landing in the back seat of my uncle's 1946 Buick. It was my mother's added misfortune to be taken to a Catholic hospital. A flurry of attendants rushed out to retrieve me, the tiny and precious cargo. My mother, her legs streaked with afterbirth, was left to walk in under her own power.

In that same year, the last few stray women were being herded back into the home from other more exotic parts of the still deliriously post-war world. Some of them knew too much and were never captured, but most, like my mother, had already broken under the pressure and surrendered. A tour through the March 1950 *Chatelaine* ("the Canadian Women's Magazine") reveals how this migration was engineered.

In this one issue, there are bright and zealous full-page advertisements for no less than four brands of washing machines, two refrigerators, an ironing machine, a kettle, floor polisher, toaster, steam iron, and the amazing "automagic sink," which converted itself into dishwasher, clothes dryer, and kitchen sink. The metal that had been needed for war machines was now being pressed into service, molded into the weapons of domestic battle.

The Beatty, "Canada's finest washer," had the famous patented "human hand" washing action; at the same time the Hotpoint boasted "instinctive wringer control." A floor polisher salesman proudly announced, "You just guide. It does all the Work." Fifteen minutes had been dropped from every ironing hour and enthusiastic house-wives everywhere were heavily endorsing GE's new Featherweight. The latest kettle could boil a pint of water in under three minutes. Why the housework was practically doing itself!

It was a giddy time all right. Even the nation's milliners sensed a shift in the wind and proclaimed, "At last fashion allows us to be frivolous in our hats again." The Tampax tampon was being heralded as "the freedom method," offering women passing through those certain days of the month release from the pin-belt-pad harness and—perhaps more importantly—"release from embarrassment and mental anxiety."

Over the next few years, the frenzy to corral women dissipated so that by early 1957, the February issue of *Chatelaine* carried not one advertisement for any appliance, major or minor. Mission had obviously been accomplished. Women were at last contained again, busy turning their creative energies homeward, engaged in the campaign for whiter whites and brighter brights. But the legacy of this time, the sense of release and sanguine optimism lived on for years. It became a part of the foundation of my life and coloured my entire childhood. I was exposed to the *promise* of it all, a naive and dizzy omnipotence. Like radiation, it seeped through the walls of my family's sad, semi-detached brick duplex.

While there was much to cheer about, the message for my mother and sisters was terribly mixed: a sinister and tangled alloy of possibility and entrapment. The subtext was that as a girl, safe passage to the promised land would come only by proxy, specifically through marriage to a man who was already there. So that while the world was my oyster, as my father was fond of saying, I myself would not be doing the actual shucking. Oh I could go out and grab a slice of life for myself, but it would have to be a small portion; hardly the booty I had been promised.

For girls, our advancement, our salvation, would come about not through any direct agency in the world, but through the rigors and discipline of self-correction and self-enhancement. This is of course where etiquette entered the picture. Why should a girl be adrift in a sea of self-improvement when she could swim to islands of safety? This is what the rules and conventions of etiquette offered: an oasis of good-breeding, a beacon, a port in the storm of impropriety to which women and girls could orient themselves.

Certainly some etiquette conventions seem to have been designed to make the world in general a more pleasant and agreeable place, but there is an undeniable emphasis on correcting women's and girls' unique defects. Almost all of these rules concerned themselves with the seemingly formidable task of making us less offensive to men; less threatening; less intelligent; less visible. Even when there are parallel chapters for women and men on the same topic of decorum, the material aimed at the female reader is nearly always much longer, more complex, more convoluted, more laced with dire warning about dire consequences. More and more text, it would seem, was needed to make women less and less of who they might be.

My mother made her own unique contribution to the "less is more" school of enhancement for girls by deciding that my eight-year-old ears should be surgically reduced in size and made to lie more neatly against the sides of my head. Although I have no doubt that she was trying in earnest to save me from the horrors of unmarriage-ability, I am haunted still by the very visceral sense that a part of my DNA lies on the cutting-room floor of good taste.

Almost forty years passed between the cropping of my ears and the moment I reached out to pick up an old book at Toronto's 1994 Hadassah Bazaar. During this time I'd become a lesbian, a banker, a feminist, and an artist. In that order. The book was called *It's More Fun When You Know the Rules: Etiquette Problems for Girls*. It was the only thing I bought that day, but it proved to be a pivotal moment of consumerism.

As I began to read the book on my flight back to Vancouver, at first I laughed at the sheer folly of it. Imagine, an entire treatise based on a kind of original sin of the female personality. But it wasn't long before I felt a deep and disturbing resonance. The book's tone of admonishment and reproach soon had the colour rising in my face, and I could feel the same hot shame I'd known as a girl, straining toward self-hood against immeasurable odds. I had never actually *seen* an etiquette book, much less read one. But now before me lay the printed words, the bald and brazen exhibitionism of a choking doctrine so perfectly internalized as to be only dimly recognized as foreign. Here at last was the source, a piece of the actual written authority that had all of my life been dispensed to me as a fine mist of innuendo, a wash of insinuation—obscured by cheerful and earnest benevolence.

One of the most insidious aspects of the message in this book and in the many others I was to find after it, is that etiquette is offered up as a legitimate path to personal freedom for girls and women.

> *Things being as they are in this world, the girl whose manners*
> *are right has more fun than the girl who isn't sure of herself*
> *and who therefore agonizes over her mistakes, and is distracted*
> *by her doubts. The girl who knows the correct thing to wear, the*
> *proper way to introduce her friends, how to eat the food that is*
> *served to her, what to say when she tells her hostess good-bye—*
> *such a girl is free really to enjoy herself.* (1935)

Through her bondage to propriety, her obsessive and desperate allegiance to detail, she is somehow made free. And not only does *she* have a better life, but she performs a kind of public service, putting all of mankind at ease:

> *Not only does the girl who knows her etiquette have more fun herself; she is more fun for her friends. They are never anxious about her making serious faux pas. When house parties or picnics or dances are being planned, someone always suggests her name. They like her because she can be counted on to do the right thing.* (1935)

And what befalls the girl who is not adequately prepared for the rigors of social life? It would seem that the failed deportment department is littered with the carcasses of young women who didn't quite know what to say, how to sit, when to leave, where to go, indeed, who to be. Again, from the same book:

> *The chances are that just when you most need it, you will forget the very thing you meant to remember. Having forgotten one thing, you will become nervous and forget something else; and soon you will be hopelessly confused and floundering.*
> (1935)

Finding this first etiquette book launched me on a mission, an obsession almost, to ferret out the words, to expose the source of the allusion; to return to the concretized form. To take the words and use them again, to claim them for myself, to turn them outward, to discharge them harmlessly into the air the way the police fire when trying not to hit any vital organs.

It has been very important for me to present the text in this 'Etiquette' body of work verbatim, exactly as it appears in the etiquette books. I wanted the times to speak for themselves, to indict themselves. I *did* arrange a slew of forced marriages with imagery from women's magazines of the same vintage, but otherwise, what you see is what we got.

Of course it could well be argued that what we got we are still getting; the messages, that is. Not much has changed except that we are ever so much more sophisticated. We even speak in terms of *post-feminism*. I think maybe the messages have just become harder to spot, laundered by liberalism, glazed over like a thanksgiving ham.

But these menacing missives still form the foundation of what it means to be a woman in white, middle- and upper-class North American culture, and while they have mutated slightly over time to become less visibly toxic, this has only driven the battle underground, deep into the tissues of anorexic girls who are literally dying to take up less space.

Just the other day I stood before a magazine counter and perused the dizzying array of choices aimed at the female reader. Like a rescue hovercraft, I plucked these headings off the covers:

"The Most Perfect Clothes" (*Allure*)
"No Mistakes Guide to Hair Colouring" (*Self*)
"10 Minutes to a Great Face" (*Mademoiselle*)

"Slim Down Fast" (*Redbook*)
"How to Fake Perfect Skin" (*Young and Modern*)
"Hair Makeovers" (*Seventeen*)
"Diary of a Facelift" (*Harpers and Queen*)
"How my Looks Shaped my Life" (*Glamour*)
"Hair Secrets" (*Look West*)
"Dress Thin Look Great" (*Ladies Home Journal*)
"Techniques to Make You Gorgeous" (*Cosmo*)
"Perfect Skin at Last" (*Elle*)
"How I lost 100 lbs: One Woman's Story" (*Toronto Life Fashion*)

Sounds rather like the business of small 's' self-improvement for girls is still thriving. And what are the boys up to? Well, judging by the covers of the rest of the magazines in the racks that day, it would seem that while the girls do the makeovers, the boys do the takeovers. And if they aren't in the board room, they are in the fields and streams, or fixing up the house, or over at the gun club. You can bet they aren't caught in a paralyzing spiral of self-examination. They take charge, they take action, and regrettably, they take the occasional moose.

But you know, there *is* hope. In spite of my mother's best intentions, and those of an entire culture, I—like a lot of women I know—am apparently impossibly ill-bred. I want my artwork to be remarked upon and openly admired. I also dash on ahead and climb into taxicabs unaided, go about looking a fright, and break down every now and then. My brains show more often than my slip, and

I have been known to start a great many conversations on subjects of interest to me. Most importantly, I make it a policy *never* to leave my personal feelings at home, or anywhere else for that matter.

List of Images

Titles of images are in the order in which the full reproductions appear. All works created in mixed media: acrylic paint, hand water-coloured laser prints and collage on paper.

Magazine images were extracted from: *Canadian Home Journal*, February 1944 and May 1946; *Chatelaine*, August 1946; *Life* , May 1954; *Saturday Evening Post*, June 1951; *Woman's Home Companion*, January 1947, June 1949 and November 1953.

Excerpts from the following sources appear integrated in the artwork and as the etiquette rules in the text:

Black, Walter J. 1940 [a]. *Elinor Ames' Book of Modern Etiquette*. New York: P. F. Collier & Son.

Eichler, Lillian. 1923. *Book of Etiquette, Vollume II*. New York: Nelson Doubleday Inc.

Fenwick, Millicent. 1948. *Vogue's Book of Etiquette: A Complete Guide to Traditional Forms and Modern Usage*. New York: Simon & Schuster.

Lane, Janet. 1947. *Your Carriage, Madam! A Guide to Good Posture*. New York: John Wiley and Sons Inc.

Pierce, Beatrice. 1935. *It's More Fun When You Know the Rules: Etiquette Problems for Girls*. New York: Farrar and Rinehart, Inc.

Post, Elizabeth L. 1965. *Emily Post's Etiquette*. New York: Funk and Wagnalls Company Inc.

Royal Canadian Air Force. 1962. *XBX Plan for Physical Fitness*. Ottawa: Queen's Printer.

Stratton, Dorothy C., and Helen B. Schleman. 1940. *Your Best Foot Forward: Social Usage for Young Moderns*. New York: McGraw-Hill Book Company, Inc.

Wilson, Margery. 1941. *Margery Wilson's Pocket Book of Etiquette: The Modern Social Guide*. New York: Pocket Books Inc.

Woodward, Elizabeth. n.d. *Ladies Home Journal* (column).

Born in Toronto in 1950, Sheila Norgate eventually migrated to the West Coast, where she settled in 1975. An ardent feminist and recovering "nice girl," she is a self-taught visual artist whose work has attracted a wide and devoted following. She has been exhibiting since 1986 and is represented in numerous private and corporate collections throughout North America. She lives in Vancouver, Canada, with her lovely partner, Martine, and their irascible cockatiel.

Press Gang Publishers has been producing vital and
provocative books by women since 1975.

SELECTED TITLES

Beyond the Pale, by Elana Dykewomon
ISBN 0-88974-074-7, PB
An epic historical novel which chronicles the personal and political journeys of
Jewish lesbians at the turn of the twentieth century.

I Am Woman, by Lee Maracle
ISBN 0-88974-059-3, PB
This new edition of Maracle's visionary book links teachings of
her First Nations heritage with feminism.

Sunnybrook: A True Story with Lies, by Persimmon Blackbridge
ISBN 0-88974-068-2, CL; ISBN 0-88974-060-7, PB
A humorous and lavishly illustrated novel about disability, mental health and passing.
Full-colour images throughout.

Cereus Blooms at Night, by Shani Mootoo
ISBN 0-88974-064-X, PB
Part magic realism, part psychological drama, this richly textured novel
explores a world where love and treachery collide.

Fire Power, by Chrystos
ISBN 0-88974-047-X, PB
Chrystos' writing has been acclaimed as "poetry which indeed changes the world."

Her Tongue on My Theory: Images, Essays and Fantasies, by Kiss & Tell
ISBN 0-88974-058-5, PB
A daring collage of explicit lesbian sexual imagery, erotic writing, personal histories and
provocative analysis.

For a complete catalogue of fiction and non-fiction, write to Press Gang Publishers,
#101-225 East 17th Avenue, Vancouver, B.C. V5V 1A6 Canada.
Or visit us online at http://www.pressgang.bc.ca/